Drawing in
Pen & Ink

Drawing in Pen & Ink

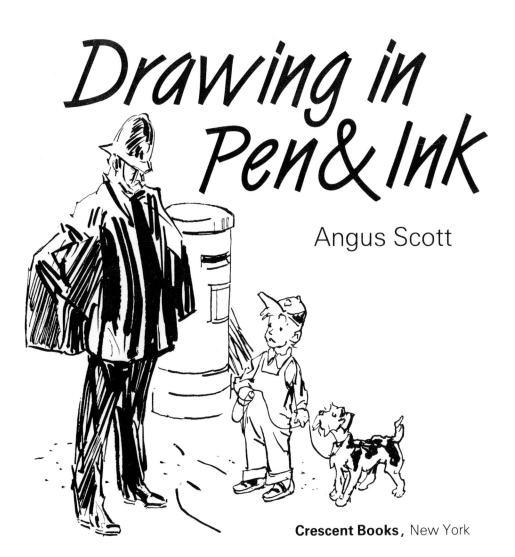

Angus Scott

Crescent Books, New York

For Eve

© Angus Scott 1985
First published 1985

1986 edition published by
Crescent Books, distributed by
Crown Publishers, Inc,

Library of Congress Cataloging-in-Publication Data

Scott, Angus.
  Drawing in pen & ink.

  1. Pen drawing—Technique. I. Title. II. Title:
Drawing in pen and ink.
NC905.S374   1986   741.2′6   85–25480
ISBN 0–517–60501–5

hgf ed cba

Contents

Preface

Of all the arts, dancing must be the most natural, for the expression is most directly translated from the mental to the physical, and surely the most unnatural must be the art of making pictures with a black line on white paper? For a start, no form in nature has a black line around it. Even half-tones are difficult to simulate with a line. Therefore, you are striving to invent a language with the line that will *remind* the spectator of the elements you have to suggest, without in any way trying to imitate their appearance as the camera does. The pen and ink artist must use every means he has to convey his message.

I remember seeing a reproduction of a very clever drawing by Leo Chaney, in which the figure of a policeman in his black cape and uniform was directing the traffic. It gave me much pleasure and, turning over the pages of the journal, an idea struck me. I went back to the drawing and, sure enough, the figure was, except for the helmet and part of the cape, snow-white, untouched paper. He had caused me to think that white was black. This is going to the limit perhaps, but it goes to show what can be done with wily use of limited resources: remember, the limitations of the medium can be used to great advantage.

If the value of drawing is not in the imitation of reality, where then does it lie? The painter Turner once said: 'Drawing is a very rummy business'. This is about as far as one can go in explaining its impulses and problems, which is really no explanation at all. If Turner could not make the meaning any clearer than that, who then could hope to explain why every child, it seems, has a naturally spontaneous desire to draw? Much better perhaps to leave the question unanswered and simply make the most of the pleasure the act of drawing gives. Rhythms and patterns are there to be sought; the flowing relationships of lines one to another; the white spaces, their sizes and shapes, and the balance between them and the black areas. Of telling importance, too, is the vitality of the line itself; coming from the power of the artist, from the mind, to the hand holding the pen or brush, and all the nervous energy that goes with it. All this to be captured and contained on the drawing paper. The artist's nature is expressed in his treatment of the subject, and the fact that no two artists are alike is what quickens the interest and holds the spectator's attention. It is like having signed your name often enough for your signature to become recognisable as your own, and, therefore, unique. So, leave imitation to the camera and *be yourself.*

There is a section of this book given to drawing the nude, and you may wonder how this can help the drawing of everyday figures seen in the streets. It does. For a better understanding of the figure inside the clothes helps to make sense of where the pen or brush lines should go on the clothed figure.

The tools of the trade: there is a wide range of nibs and brushes available and, as interpretation is a personal matter, so the tools you choose will determine your style, which is what the endeavour is all about – the unique expression of the artist.

1 Materials and techniques

To begin with, a soft pencil and a pocket sketch-book are your first needs. Use a 3B pencil brought to a very long point, shaving the lead needle sharp. Always draw from reality rather than from photographs. A camera can be useful sometimes, but do not rely on it too heavily. A photograph can be useful if you are called upon by an editor to do a very quick drawing of an unusual scene – the interior of a submarine, or a South American Casino for example – clearly you have to get your information from somewhere – but the pencil drawing from life is always worth a hundred photographs, and I am speaking from the experience of a lifetime. Here then are the tools you will need:

1 A 3B pencil, a sharp knife and a rubber for cleaning off the pencil marks after inking-in.

2 A sketch-book of the clip, loose-leaf type; its stiff back will serve as a drawing board.

3 A flexible nib. There is a large range to choose from – a Gillot 303 is a good, lively nib.

4 A relief nib. This is the smallest size in lettering pens and is useful in getting a clean, decorative line. You will also need a small piece of rag to wipe the pen nibs.

5 A ball-point pen (black) gives a very fast line, does not splutter round corners, but runs freely in any direction. It does not, however, have the character of the 303 nib.

6 A small, sable water-colour brush, No. 2. Make sure you wash it after use: this is an expensive investment, and the ink would destroy it if allowed to dry. You might also try a No. 0 brush (the smallest of all). Do not feel tied to these nib suggestions. If they suit you, well and good, if not, keep on experimenting until you feel comfortable with your tools.

7 A mirror for making studies of your own hands, in the absence of a model.

8 Apart from the sketch-book, Bristol board is the ideal thing for pen and ink drawing: its surface allows you to clean or scrape off gently any errors or corrections that you want to make.

9 A bottle of black Indian ink (waterproof).

10 A half-pound jar of Process White. You may use this for blotting out errors if the drawing is intended for reproduction and not for exhibition.

Another item you ought to acquire, is the smallest of folding seats. You can concentrate much better, and save a lot of time and energy if you can sit instead of stand to do your sketches. It is little bigger than your sketch-book, and so light that both can be folded under your arm quite comfortably.

Accidents will happen. A slight nudge of the ink-well and you can ruin a whole day's work. Believe me, it happens. So, take a flat cardboard cigarette packet and cut out a hole in the lid thus.

Gillot 303 nib. A nib giving a fine hair-line, but capable of strong breadth of line.

The 'J' nib. The smallest lettering pen, which gives a hard line and is useful if you want to give an outline to inanimate objects. It can be used also for flat patterns if need be. It is different from the flexible nib. Experiment with it and you will see how it can be.

A fine ball-point. This is different again from the other nibs in that it can move very fast around corners without having to leave the paper, and can turn back on itself, which no other nib can do. Useful for very speedy notes and sketches indoors and outdoors. It comes in a range of colours but insist on black, as you may want to reproduce the sketches one day.

The No. 1 Sable brush. Gives from a fine to a very broad line, and is useful for filling in the larger areas of black.

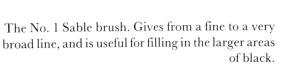

Here are some preliminary scribbles with the tools of your trade, to get the feel of the various types of line that are possible. To show the strong unyielding line of the relief nib, I have drawn the two cars in this simple, diagram-like way, but in one car I used the 303 nib for the finest lines to help suggest the glint in the top of the car: for everything else I used the 303 nib. Notice especially the wide range of this nib in the S-shaped line at the top of the left-hand corner. For the large blobs of black, I used the small sable brush. For this kind of practice, I am a firm advocate of speed in putting the ink lines down, but think carefully while it is still in pencil, before you commit yourself in ink.

A flexible 303 nib liner for the figure (head, body, legs and newspaper). Note the S-shaped line on her hair, starting fine and widening with pressure on the nib, and the altered character of the line on the wall panel with the same nib.

A relief nib for the telephone-table and the outline of the chair. A strong, hard, unyielding line.

A No. 1 sable brush for the rug, black skirt, and the blobs on the chair pattern, covering big areas very quickly.

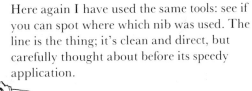

Here again I have used the same tools: see if you can spot where which nib was used. The line is the thing; it's clean and direct, but carefully thought about before its speedy application.

13

Doodles this time with a fine ball-point (black ink). A flexible nib needs coaxing in the direction desired and the constant dipping in the ink-well makes speed impossible, whereas the ball-point gives a characterless, but very fast line. These doodles are from the blank spaces in my telephone book. They may seem nonsensical but they keep the hand mobile. One day, the postman came to change the telephone directories and as I gave him the old ones he glanced at the covers back and front. Seeing the doodles he smiled and said, 'We keep these bits' – so at least they must mean something to someone.

By the way, these really are doodles, but it is only by constant practice that facility comes.

Cross-hatching always seems to me to be a very awkward treatment. It is striving for half-tones in a way unnatural to line. Every line on your drawing should have a full right to exist with its unspoiled character to make its contribution to the whole. In cross-hatching, the lines seem to be at odds with each other, only to cancel each other out. Differing shades should be arrived at by other means.

In these small sketches you will see dark tones suggested alongside darker tones: the lines will move, where necessary, in different directions, and vary from fine to heavy, but they will never clash with one another. The smallest line has its own special contribution. Examine them, if you like, through a magnifying glass and you will see that this is so. Note the fine line of the 303 nib on the nose of the old head at the top and contrast it with the bold use of the No. 1 brush on the figure of the nun.

Here is a sketch-book opportunity: a sleeping beggar by the side of the road
who slept long enough for me to catch what you see here and, with a
model's fee in this tin, both he and I were very satisfied. I have used it, as
it shows the usefulness of splatterwork and, unlike the blockmaker's tint,
you can achieve this effect for yourself. To achieve the grey effect around his
head and shoulders I first cut out a mask in paper to shield the parts which
I wished to remain white, then wet a tooth-brush with black ink and
splatted the ink over the unshielded area by drawing a knife gently across
the wet bristles. Sketched in quickly with a 3B pencil and inked in later with
a flexible nib and a No. 1 brush for the strong blobs.

2 Using the Sketch-book

Skill does not come by itself, it needs to be worked upon. There is always a discipline involved before one can become adept at anything. For example, the reader who is too lazy to go for a dictionary will always remain in the dark when he comes to a word with which he is unfamiliar. To the student who has the habit of finding out, it becomes an impossibility *not* to haul himself out of the armchair and get the information he needs. So it is with drawing. You should carry your pocket sketch-book wherever you go so that even on a bus, for example, you will learn always to see something upon which you can practise. The habit of getting out your sketch-book and drawing *something*, even if it is only a case on a luggage rack, will become a necessity, and you will be angry and frustrated if you find yourself without pencil and paper. Cultivate this good habit.

Your beginnings might be so poor that you might think there's not much point in continuing, but do not give in to this: just keep going, and the quick action lines which you put down will get better and better – after all, the concert pianist would never reach that level if he did not make his fingers go: he expects to make mistakes to start with.

The sketches in this chapter are, with the exception of the pony on p.28, of static objects – machinery, buildings and countryside scenes. They are all quickly executed with the minimum of lines, in odd moments, but there is a little more time to study the subject than with moving figures, which will be considered in the following chapter.

How many times have I had a sub-editor standing over me at my drawing easel, rustling galley proofs, anxiously looking for a drawing that I have not even begun. Drawing very fast, and exasperated for having taken on the job, I know that what I will produce will be good enough, but alas, good enough is really not acceptable. The hours of practice, and my pile of sketch-books stand me in very good stead at such times.

I drop my wife off to go shopping and, whilst waiting for her, out comes the sketch-book. There are only a few minutes before we move again, only time for a few quick lines, but there is the best part of a pub in my sketch-book – much more profitable than just sitting and doing nothing. I once saw a taxi driver in Fleet Street at the busiest time of day reading his newspaper on the steering wheel while waiting for the lights to change. It would be going too far to fix your sketch-book to the steering wheel but, short of this, let nothing stop your enthusiasm.

This drawing measures only 4 x 2 in., but what a way to ward off boredom while waiting at the wheel! Perhaps about 10 minutes on this one, and inked in afterwards.

In this scene it seems that the new buildings have appeared suddenly like strangers among the old familiars in the morning sun, and I feel the need to get something down on paper. The results in the sketch-book do not come without some discomfort, for it is a cold morning and my fingers are nipped with the frost. Speed is the thing but, however short the time, you will always capture something of the spirit of the scene. Study it for a moment at home, and ink it in with lively and direct lines. Remember, the line and it's direct freshness are what are most important. The bold broad lines on the foreground tree were drawn with the 303 nib.

These little cameos do not take more than 10 or 15 minutes to do and they are fun as well as being instructive. The subjects are all around you: take them home and ink them in.

This was from an old sketch-book. I don't remember doing it, except that
it was on one of my visits to Paris. My point is that when I draw in my
sketch-book (unless it is for some specific purpose) I do not dwell on each
item but get on with the next thing that takes my attention. Although I may
seem quite to forget what I have done, the lesson has sunk into the
subconscious just the same, and nothing gets lost.

My attention was caught here by the peculiar door-knocker, and the whole thing was sketched in 15 minutes at most. It might well be useful information in the future for an illustration. But, in any case, it was an interesting doorway to examine, and very good practice in keeping the pencil flying.

This is the usually unexplored back view of a country pub; well worth a 15 minute stop. And I learned something about where all the picturesque debris goes!

Here is another pleasant exterior, with the movements of the tree considered in relation to the beam-support and the direction of the shadow line. Note also the value of the blacks in the right place on the windows.

Here an overgrown and obviously little used
entrance to the church ground, drawn so that the
focal point is encased by the heavy, encircling
movement of the foliage at the top, which comes
over and down to meet the rising swirl of grass
below on the left. This leads the eye into the
image of the building as do the dark lines of the
broken fence at the top of the steps. Perhaps
about 20 minutes were spent on this one, inked in
with 303 nib and a No. 1 brush for the large
blacks.

It always surprises me that people can find so
many ways of wasting time. Once at a garden
party I found that I was doing just that, so I
slipped away and found the farm side of the
place. There was an old barn and a pony in the
paddock and, having my sketch-book with me as
always, I soon became most pleasantly occupied
and had something to show for my day. And
when I got back to the party, no one had even
noticed my absence. If you want to gain facility
with the pencil *don't waste time;* catch every
movement.

On a steep rise in a secluded part of the garden I found this all but derelict
barn. Perhaps the 10 or 15 minutes spent would give me enough reference
for a future illustration, and at least it was keeping my pencil in practice.

On this sketch, I must confess, a little more time was spent. The pony was
on the move and so I had to do a number of speedy impressions; I chose this
one, as the old barn and the trees behind add more interest to the sketch.

3 Moving figures— catching the essence

When sketching, remember it's the line that is important. It comes from within and is part of one's character in the way that handwriting is. Our experiences and practice with the pen makes it come through the finger ends to the nib and on to the paper. This is what makes every artist different; it is the peculiar expression of the individual and this is where the value of art lies; it is always entertaining. There is absolutely nothing haphazard in the use of the pen; each stroke should be carefully considered before being laid on, however speedily. Where possible, these sketches have been reproduced actual size to show better what the line is made of, as something of this is always lost in reduction. It is like a poor recording of a well-played piece of music – we recognise the tune, but something of the colour is lost.

In the following pages are some quick sketches of figures captured in everyday situations – on the bus, in the café, at the village fete, etc. One word of caution: before you begin drawing, see *big.* For, if you spend too much time on detail your model may well have moved or vanished completely before your drawing is finished. Go for the broad movements and, with constant practice, your perceptions will sharpen, and skill with the pencil will follow. Make all the mistakes there are: your sketches will only improve by practice. Do not destroy them, but keep them and watch for your improvement and, whether or not you are pleased with what you have done, still make a point of inking them in.

They may not be fashion models, but it's a wet day and inside the bus they are something to draw. Don't waste time. Get what you can in your sketch-book and ink it in at home. Don't forget touches like the cigarette between the fingers: it all adds to an expression of a type.

Who was he? I don't know. Just someone seen on the bus. I show this drawing to make a point – *leave it to your eyes*. Everyone is in agreement, for instance, that the human nose comes to a round end. You will see that this one did not, but finished in a perpendicular line. Yet it is curiously convincing. If I had stopped to consider my knowledge, or rather what I thought I knew, of the human face, I should have rejected the information which my eyes gave me, and drawn something other than what you see here. Our eyes do not deceive us: it is we ourselves who alter the message that they give us. Leave it to your eyes and your hands will do the rest.

In this quick movement, how simple the line. You will get nothing but back views in a bus, but they are better than no models at all, and there is always something new to be seen in the different hair and hat styles.

Here, in the garden, the flash of a figure. The figure is always seen in the broadest of terms, and down it goes, right or wrong, and you are on the way to getting something of value.

Here again with just a few pencil lines you may surprise yourself in getting, if not a portrait (which is not what you are after anyway), an effect of a figure in the sunlight, busy at something. This must be the work of a minute, so every second counts. Remember that it is the broad, simple action that you are after, drawn with a 3B pencil and inked in afterwards.

Your sketch-book is in your pocket and you have spotted a good action figure. Ask the model to hold the pose for just two minutes, and be as speedy as you can (you might be able to steal an extra few seconds). This is as much as you can hope to get, but the general lively movement is well worth while and of great value for inking in afterwards.

In the park. Following this figure and drawing at the same time, would seem to be a difficult thing to attempt, but try it and surprise yourself.

You cannot get everything drawn at this speed. I managed to get the direction of his right arm but not the folds. Perhaps I wasted time in drawing his wristwatch and bootlaces.

The baby fidgeted a lot, but the thumb-in-mouth was well worth catching.

Try not to let the model become aware of what you are doing. Figures engrossed in conversation are best and, even then, you need to be pretty sly and speedy to get away with it.

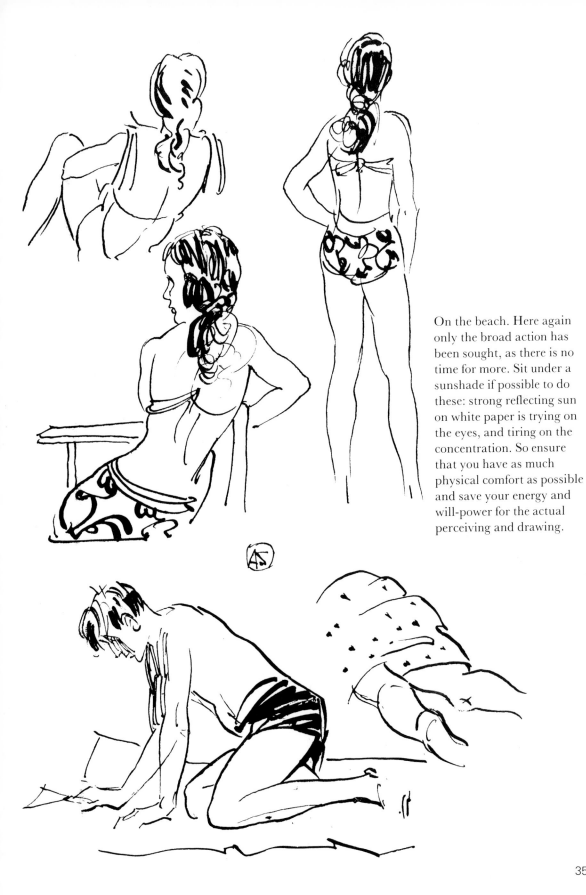

On the beach. Here again
only the broad action has
been sought, as there is no
time for more. Sit under a
sunshade if possible to do
these: strong reflecting sun
on white paper is trying on
the eyes, and tiring on the
concentration. So ensure
that you have as much
physical comfort as possible
and save your energy and
will-power for the actual
perceiving and drawing.

The models in these situations will be too engrossed in getting a sun-tan to pay any attention to what you are doing.

A very few lines can suggest a lot. For example, although the pram could not get much attention, the action of the legs of the mother was well worth catching. You will always catch something, but you must be speedy. Many people suffer a kind of embarrassment when drawing with people around. Visitors at the village fete, or anywhere else where there is plenty of movement and things to be seen, are not interested very much in what you are doing. They might give you a passing glance but that is all, so don't feel in any way shy, for you will soon become accustomed to concentrating on your drawing while excluding all else.

Throw these darts as quickly as possible and, even if at first you miss the target, you will eventually begin to get closer. Even if it is only a slight advance, you are adding a little more to your knowledge. There is plenty of ammunition – pencil and paper. Ink them in afterwards, even the bad ones, with pen and No. 1 brush – all good practice.

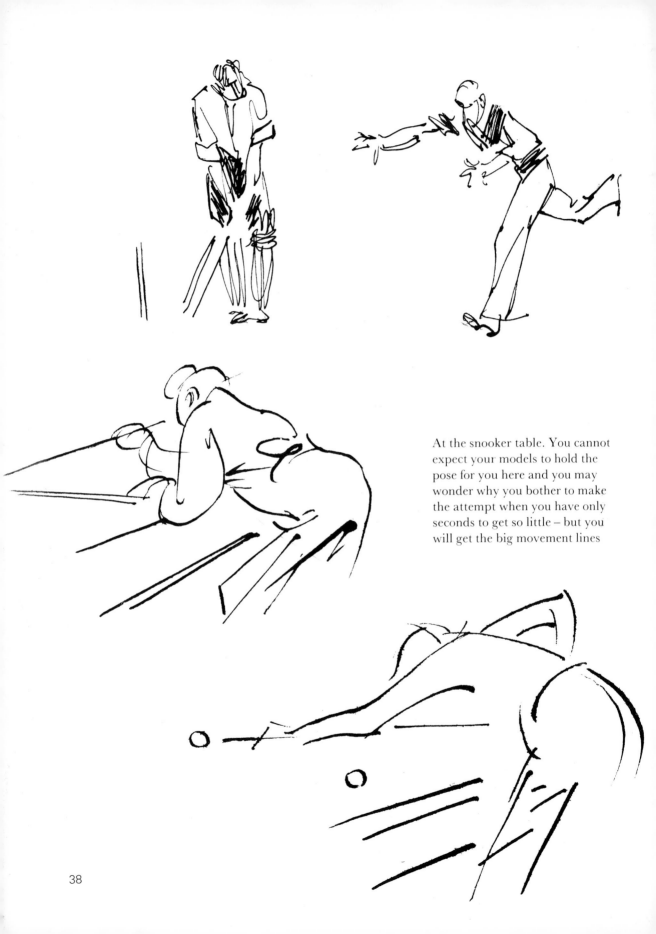

At the snooker table. You cannot
expect your models to hold the
pose for you here and you may
wonder why you bother to make
the attempt when you have only
seconds to get so little – but you
will get the big movement lines

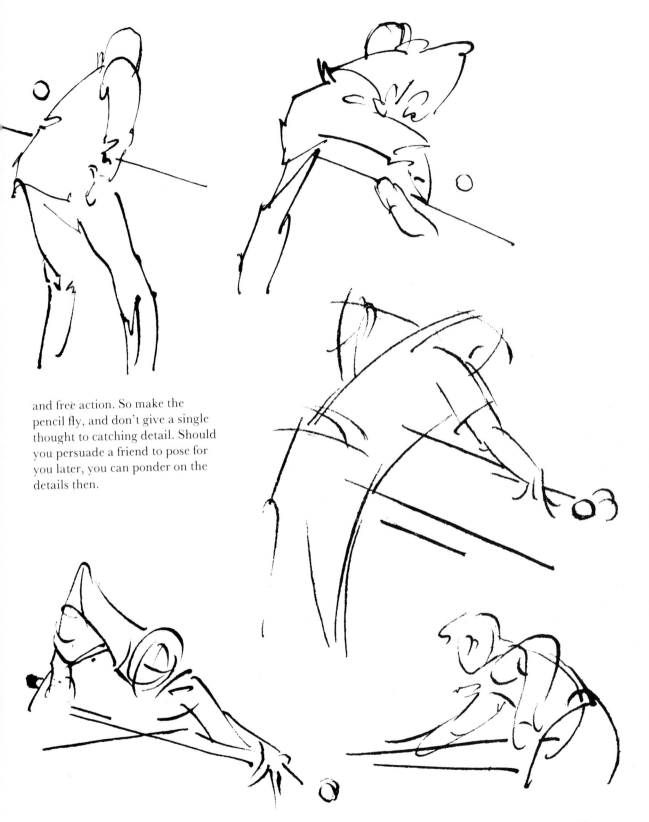

and free action. So make the
pencil fly, and don't give a single
thought to catching detail. Should
you persuade a friend to pose for
you later, you can ponder on the
details then.

If there is a very small space of time for drawing what you see at the snooker table, then there is no time at all for figures on the football field. So, since these attitudes cannot be had from posed figures, you are left only with your own quick observation and memory, coupled with the experience that constant sketch-book practice will bring. These action lines are very simply drawn, but form a basis from which to produce more detailed figures.

Here, some of these simple attitude suggestions have been carried further, and put together to make finished arrangements. In creating a new pattern, by the way, you would be lucky to find

photographs that would answer to your needs.
So you might have to juggle with figures this way
and that in small rough sketches until they
became unified into a strong whole.

I once had occasion to go to Hameln with my sketch-book and, on the way, boarded the train at Hanover. With an hour to wait, I made some quick pencil sketches in the streets. Here is one of a traffic policeman. He became aware that he was under scrutiny and, although I was sorry for his puzzlement, I continued to sketch him. I did not stay for more than a few minutes and left with a record of an interesting figure.

The two sketches of Paris streets were done some years
ago, judging by the age of the cars. It sometimes calls for
some resolution to draw in public with people bustling
around you and your model becoming more inquisitive
by the minute, so you must draw quickly with a steady
hand and a cool head and ignore everything around you.

4 Studies of hands

It has been truly said that if you can draw hands, you can draw anything. For this reason the student must make the most serious study of hands. A good practice is to get a hand mirror and spend an hour every day studying your hands. Two mirrors would be even better, one reflecting the other.

Draw your hands from all angles and all sides. Change their position and change the lighting if possible: strengthen the shadow effects to assist your modelling.

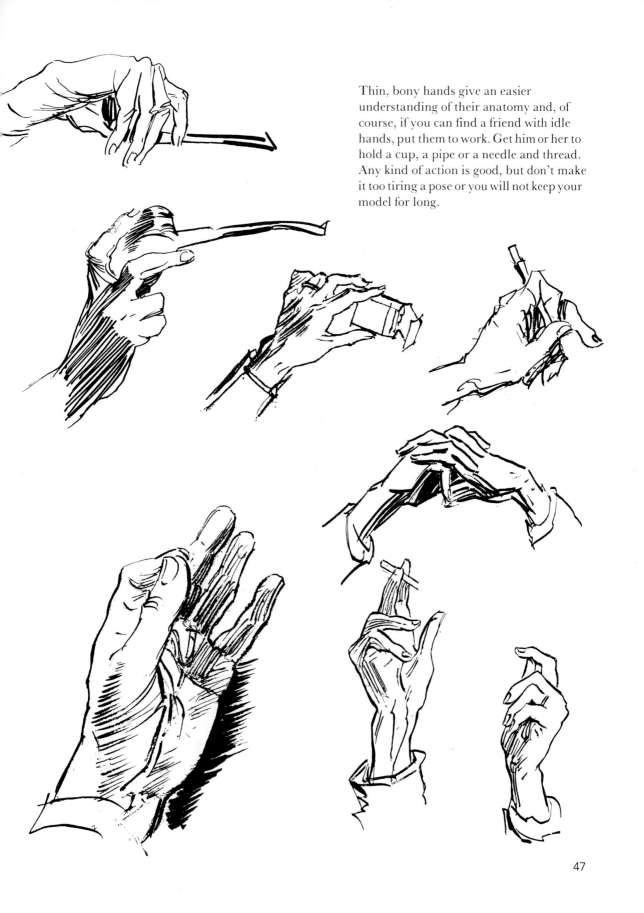

Thin, bony hands give an easier understanding of their anatomy and, of course, if you can find a friend with idle hands, put them to work. Get him or her to hold a cup, a pipe or a needle and thread. Any kind of action is good, but don't make it too tiring a pose or you will not keep your model for long.

Some more hands relative to the head. Do not bother about getting a portrait in these studies, it is the hands, after all, that you are anxious about and their relationship to the head.

5 Quick sketches of animals

I have often heard people say: 'There is nothing to draw here.' I cannot understand this: there is always something at hand, and when you get bored with the television, look around you. Household pets make readily available subject matter. There is the cat asleep on the rug: draw him while he is still, and catch him quickly in his movements when he wakes. You should not use photographs for these exercises, but use your eyes and look for information in the live model. This way you will react to your own sensations and so your own 'handwriting' will develop: do not expect to borrow your feelings from the camera.

If you can draw the cat often enough from life, quick comic inventions like these two characters will come as second nature. Do them by the score and do not be ashamed of them – keep covering the paper. Ultimately you will be doing more good ones than bad, and you should keep them all to mark your progress.

Some very quick movements for the cat action. Remember, you have only seconds in which to catch these movements, *not minutes*. Only on the sketch of the head of the sleeping cat was I allowed minutes because he was asleep, but I was just as speedy in case he woke up. As you see, I inked them in later. The cat lying down remained still long enough to be drawn more carefully and inked in later with a fine pen and brush.

Notice, too, the top cat on the left and how the pads on his paws are
arranged.

Here are three finished drawings of cats. Note the dry brush effect on the cat's head, contrasting with the fine pen lines on his back. In the sketch of the sleeping cat I suggested the outline of the cat by making the pressure on the nib start heavily from the cat and taper finely outwards. Do not start from outwards with a fine line pressing towards the cat. As grass grows from the base, draw the cat's fur that way: it's the natural way to get the effect.

It should always be a pleasure to draw, but sometimes will-power and the last ounce of energy are called for when you see something which ought to be drawn. On one occasion I had been on the road since 5.30 a.m. – all the way from Sussex to Ayrshire. Climbing wearily up to my hotel bedroom at nearly midnight, I found a Great Dane asleep on my bed. After the surprise, I thought to ring for the porter, but instead, very quietly so as not to wake the dog, got out my sketch-book and made this drawing. Never having examined a Great Dane before, I was interested to draw one for the first time, and how surprising were his paws seen from underneath. What had started as a duty soon became a pleasure, and I forgot my fatigue.

These were somewhat more
easily found models. There is
usually a dog around of some
kind, be it St Bernard, Alsation,
chihuahua or mongrel. Do not
draw a continuous outline
around the model but fix the
limits in space in your mind's
eye at intervals here and there.
These short-hand notations
will give you the broad
proportions.

6 Boats and harbours

Now for a change of scene. This time a subject that may be less familiar to many than the previous examples, and quite unlike the quick action lines of live models. These new images may call for some contemplation, but the adjustment is good for the eye and hand. Even if you do not understand the structures of the unfamiliar, accurate perception and constant drawing practice will bring an understanding and sympathy for the objects and, even though you may not intend to specialise in seaside subjects, the exercise will strengthen your drawing skill.

Here, in this harbour scene, the toothbrush stipple has been used to good effect (*see also p. 16*).

Another harbour scene,
capturing the fascinating
lines of these little boats.

A simple arrangement made
from a few derelict rowing
boats and a boat in the
middle distance. Even the
cloud shape adds to the
pattern as a whole.
Simplicity and the line itself
are what are important here.

A figure whom I caught painting his boat. How
it begins: judge with the eye the first few simple
lines which will set the scale and the subdivisions
will fall into place easily.

PUBLIC HARD

An attitude well worth catching.
By leaving it to the eye, the
placing of the elbow comes out
just right.

Another type of boat, suggested in
the simplest possible way with the
pen and the brush for the heavy
lines.

7 Drawing from 'life'

If you ever have the opportunity to do some figure drawing from a live model, as in the following pages, you should do so. You may have some difficulty in finding where to go for this facility, but there are, all over the country, a great number of reputable art groups who club together to engage models, sharing the cost, if only for one evening a week. It is still as good a way of improving your drawing today as it was for the ancient Greeks.

Perhaps the quickest way of finding such an art group, would be to go to the nearest school where evening classes are held. Join the art class there, and enquire of the tutor where such a group might be found. As the art tutor himself is invariably a professional artist he will be able to put you in touch with the most likely prospect. There are in the region of 50,000 artists in the country, and although by far the greater are amateur painters, they are all equally sincere about what they are doing. These are the most likely people to approach about the engaging of models. Every fair-sized town has its group of artists and enthusiasts – where there's a will, there's a way.

If there is a natural history museum in the vicinity a very useful preparation to drawing figures is to study the human skeleton: draw it and see how it articulates. Not a very pleasant subject for your pencil, you may think, but the discipline is good for you, and will repay you well with a keener understanding of how the human figure moves. The more you draw it, the more interesting it will become, and the satisfaction in your drawings will override all other reactions. You will find that an appreciation of the human skeleton will also help with your drawings of animals and birds. On the outside there may be little resemblance between a man and a horse, but, so far as the inside structure is concerned, all animals and birds are related.

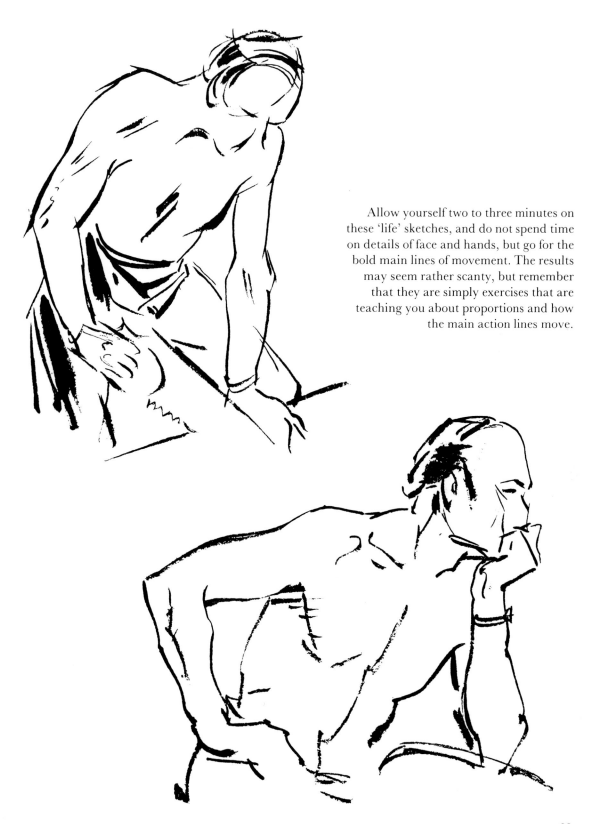

Allow yourself two to three minutes on these 'life' sketches, and do not spend time on details of face and hands, but go for the bold main lines of movement. The results may seem rather scanty, but remember that they are simply exercises that are teaching you about proportions and how the main action lines move.

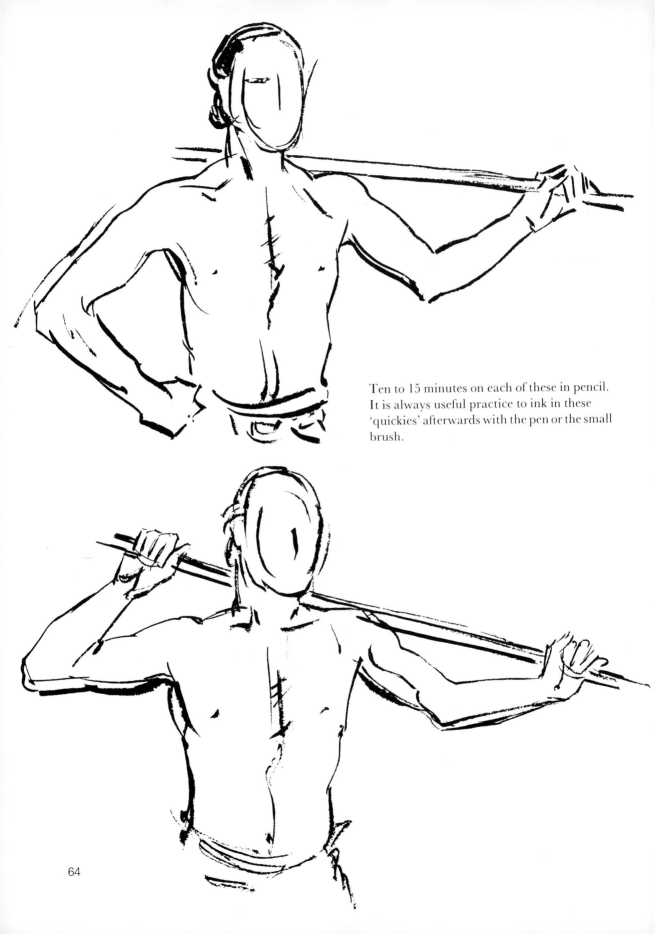

Ten to 15 minutes on each of these in pencil. It is always useful practice to ink in these 'quickies' afterwards with the pen or the small brush.

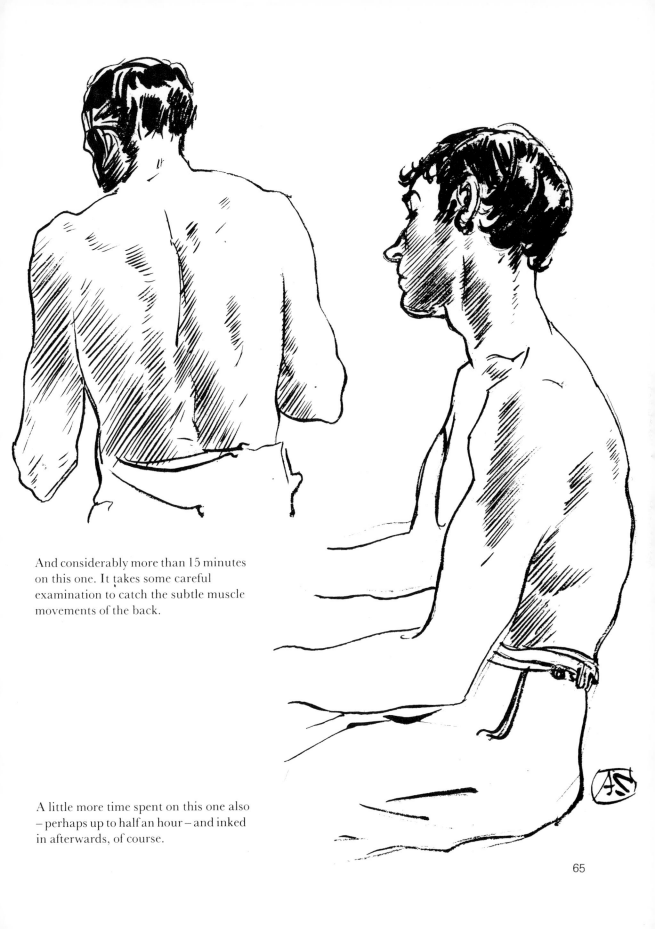

And considerably more than 15 minutes
on this one. It takes some careful
examination to catch the subtle muscle
movements of the back.

A little more time spent on this one also
– perhaps up to half an hour – and inked
in afterwards, of course.

Here, an opportunity to use one
patient model – yourself. Get in
front of a long mirror and draw.
Remember the mirror studies of
your own hands?

Although a little more time was spent on the figure on the right, the action of the left-hand figure is still there and, as with the other drawings, the use of the carbon pencil is a great help with the soft modelling.

Here is an easy pose for the model. Drawn with a 4B pencil and
strengthened with the carbon pencil for the shadows in the modelling and
in the head.

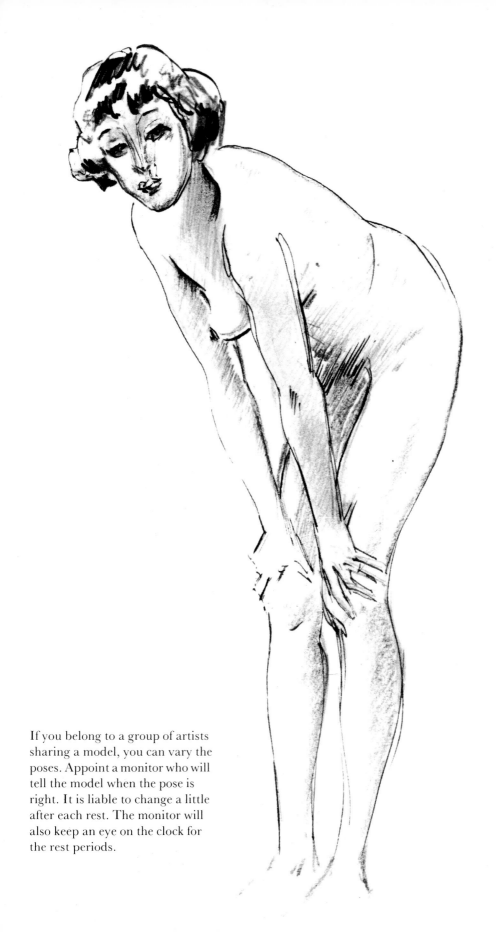

If you belong to a group of artists
sharing a model, you can vary the
poses. Appoint a monitor who will
tell the model when the pose is
right. It is liable to change a little
after each rest. The monitor will
also keep an eye on the clock for
the rest periods.

You will find that there is always a friend who will be willing to pose for the odd occasion at home. Do not make them sit for too long. People are not (apart from professional models) accustomed to sit quite still for much more than 15 minutes at a stretch. Give amateur models plenty of rests or you will not keep them long. This drawing was inked in with a fully loaded No. 1 brush for the coat, but a semi-dry brush dragged on for the shadows on the face and hair.

A speedy effort this, in 15 minutes, with the carbon pencil again in use for the soft shadow effect, but no time allowed for the hands and feet.

It makes a stimulating change for the eye to have a costumed model. Here is a dancer in her outfit, holding a pose which is not difficult to maintain. She might easily stay like this without movement for well over the half-hour.

The 'life' class group might, for a change, decide to have a time limit of 10 to 15 minutes to a drawing, so that each artist can change his angle for a new image of the pose. Here is an example of a 15-minute sketch. There is no time for detail, but it does catch the action, and helps the appreciation of proportions.

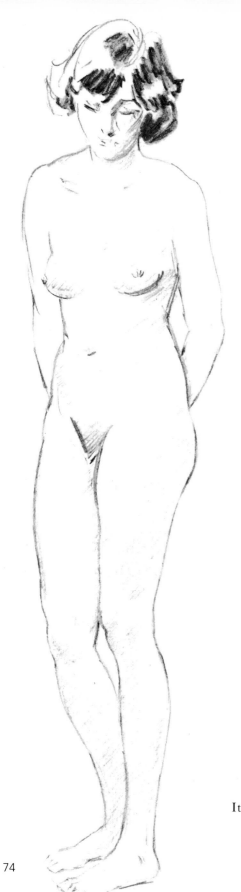

It would take a two-hour session of posing to carry a drawing this far, giving the model a rest of five minutes every half hour.

A drawing from another two-hour session. The shading was suggested with a carbon pencil. It produces a particularly soft and sympathetic effect. You will notice here and there a sharpening of the outline, which was achieved with the black ink and 303 nib.

Some 'life' studies go more easily than others and this one was one of those. It is an unpredictable exercise, but it demands sharp concentration at all times. Carbon pencil effects again strengthened with pen outline. If you do not feel the need to sharpen your drawings in this way, don't do it: you are free to follow your own feelings. If you want to use a 4B pencil from start to finish and nothing else, do so. After all, it is the drawing itself that counts in the long run.

A study of the subtlety of movements of the
back muscles. This is not an easy exercise and
demands careful scrutiny and intense
concentration: how useful again is the soft
gradation of the carbon pencil. The contours
are sharpened again with the pen nib.

A little more time spent on this one than on some of the others, shaded with the carbon pencil and a penned outline. By the way, your finished pencil drawings should be sprayed with a fixative to prevent smudging. The same applies to drawings done with charcoal, pastel, crayon or chalk.

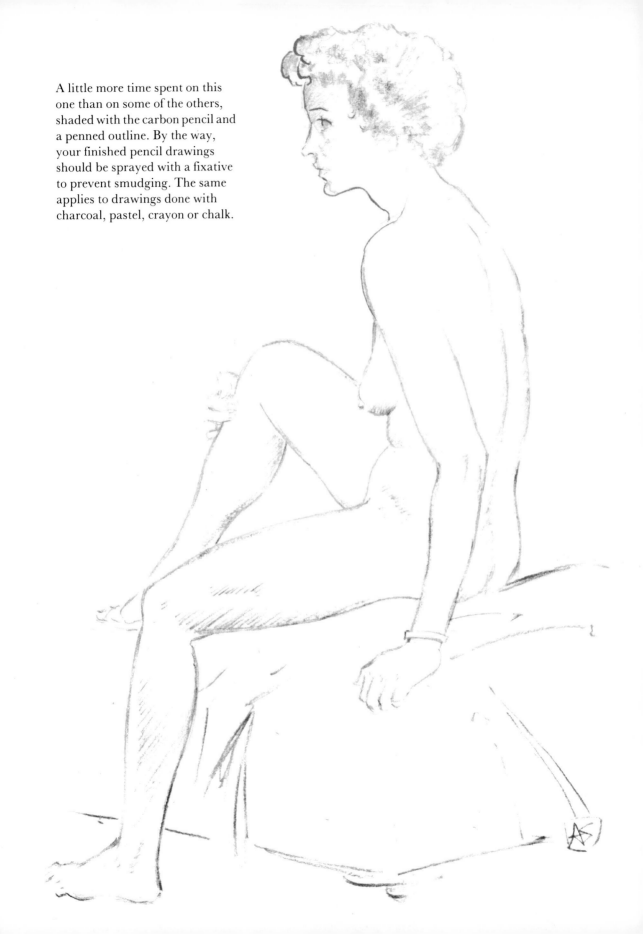

8 The discipline of research - on the farm

I read a critic's report in one of the glossy magazines not so long ago of an exhibition of paintings which he had visited. He had asked the artist about one of the paintings in particular and the artist explained that he had kept the painting for two years before he recognised what the subject was, and had then given it a title. I am glad to say that the critic spoke his mind about that. Whilst the abstract undoubtedly has its value as an art form, products of the subconscious may often have no obvious message to convey at all and may even cover up a distinct lack of talent. The pen and ink artist, however, must know sharply and clearly what he is trying to do, for, although the ability to draw is a great gift, the artist is giving away his very nature with every line that he puts down, so he must be honest. Whichever direction he decides to follow, whether it be large, solemn paintings, pretty landscapes, or light illustrations such as the fun of cartoons and comic strips, it is daily practice with the sketch-book that will give him the confidence to say what he means in his own individual way. If he has problems, he must work out the answers sincerely, and this means going back to life for understanding – above all, his work should be the spontaneous reaction to what he sees.

The following two studies of horses at work involved a considerable amount of research and the collecting together of numerous details about horses, ploughs and timber-waggons before attempting the final picture.

These small shorthand notes may seem to be just so many meaningless trifles, and indeed each note by itself may have very little meaning, but all added together could help realise a logical whole.

First of all, some studies of the plough-horse itself to be matched up with the plough later. This sleepy horse resting at midday with his companion, gave me a good chance to look at the collar and the odd bits of chain and rope. Incidentally, when the farmer saw this sketch he said 'That's Clansman all right, he's bone idle.' So, without knowing that, and relying entirely on what my eyes told me I had managed to get across accurately his character. Don't ponder over what you see, don't question, just draw it.

Sleepy Clansman again, from the other side, with more enlightenment about the collar and the parts around his mouth and head. The slightest change in the angle reveals new understanding. I had to go around the horse to see better how the collar was constructed. Inevitably, the horse will get less attention than usual in the quick examination of the straps, buckles and chains. This can be a very puzzling study, so that many quick notes might be necessary before an understanding of their function comes.

The horse all dressed up at a ploughing contest, too, can look very different from his usual workaday appearance. Here, the horse has been released from the plough, and the chains and ropes hang loose, but closer scrutiny is needed to know how they work, and more information can be learned from other angles. Nothing can be done without knowledge, so take pains in the sketch-book.

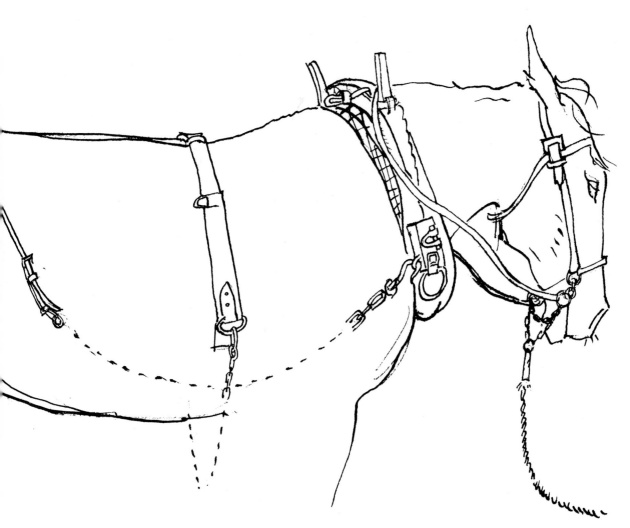

In the stable it is very difficult to get anything other than rear views, but
these are better than nothing. Here you see a glimpse of ploughing horses
in their stalls. Do not worry about getting the whole animal in this time. It
is something to be able to understand the weight and power of their
hindquarters.

Here is a peep at one aspect of the stables. This kind of background information is never wasted, although it may not be used in the final picture; it all helps build up the artist's sympathy and an understanding of the subject.

A lucky encounter, and a change for a moment from the heavier horses. A mother and her foal – well worth the few minutes it takes to put them into the sketch-book.

In this sketch notice the blockmaker's tint, used for a shadow on the horses. The area that you want shaded by the blockmaker may be suggested on your drawing with a thin watercolour wash of Prussian Blue.

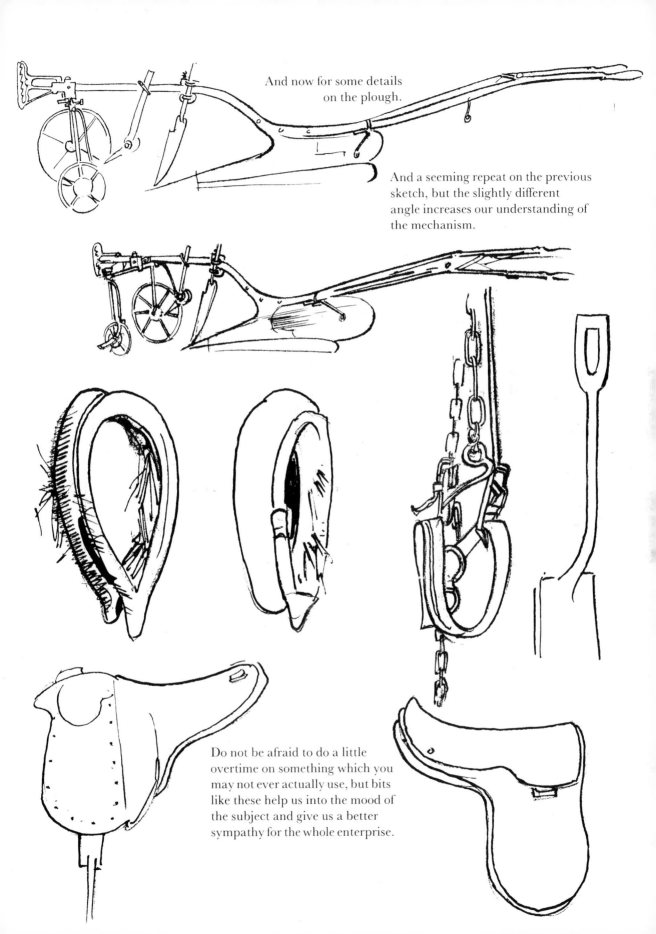

And now for some details
on the plough.

And a seeming repeat on the previous
sketch, but the slightly different
angle increases our understanding of
the mechanism.

Do not be afraid to do a little
overtime on something which you
may not ever actually use, but bits
like these help us into the mood of
the subject and give us a better
sympathy for the whole enterprise.

These quick little notes will help you to check on what you think you remember: even the merest hint of something can clear away a doubt now and then. We can do nothing without information.

Left These sketches took no more than ten minutes each and I set a limit round them with a line which helped to contain the image in my mind. I used a black horse against a grey, giving a valuable 'punch' in contrast. This first rough makes a good little composition and, even if I don't use it this time, I may well do on some other occasion. So, do not destroy anything – everything comes in useful sooner or later.

The vitality of the first rough sketch is very often tempting enough to use for publication, but try to do the drawing again, using the information you have gained in your quest for knowledge re the horse equipment. At the same time you must try to put back the vitality of the first sketch which is not always easy to do. In this second rough I have used the heavy cloud on the left to help balance the dark areas on the bottom right, and the invention of the sky pattern binds the whole.

An attempt at a finished drawing here, using the first rough.

In the end, I went back to the second little rough after all. As you see, much of the information gathered on the plough has been abandoned for the sake of the whole effect. A lot of ploughing detail would have been somehow irrelevant, but it was necessary to know it before discarding it.

The second drawing I wanted to do was of horses pulling a timber-waggon
and this, too, involved a hunt for information. What does a timber-waggon
look like? It is necessary to find out. But first, a few more glimpses of horses.

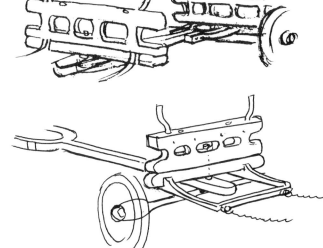

On a remote farm I found the remains of what once had been a timber-cart. It was in the middle of a spinney, thickly overgrown and almost invisible from some aspects. It had heeled over, as two of the wheels had parted from the main structure, quite decayed and broken up and buried under wild growth. First I had to clear some space around it, so I borrowed a bagging-hook from the farmer. How did it look so long ago? I had to do some detective work on what was left of it and rebuild it again on my sketch-pad. Here, then, are the drawings at which I finally arrived.

Here is the finished drawing, built up from the information collected on the timber waggon and horses. However, do not neglect any suspicion that there might be a little more to be had from the subject – even a slight improvement is always worth the trouble and is good for discipline.

And here another treatment of the woodland in the background. I felt that the new line movements of the trees give an extra liveliness to the whole effect. It is a good idea, if time permits, to put a drawing aside and not look at it for a few days, to allow for second thoughts. The subconscious mind will often come up with an improved idea.

9 Book illustration

In the following pages are some thoughts on illustrating. New editions of the classics of every period are always appearing which call for considerable research by the artist as to costumes, modes and manners. Although there is a lot of pleasure in drawing, there is also discipline. You may never want to draw period figures but, whatever your chosen subject, you must stir yourself to find out what things are made of and how they look. Know how is fine, but you must also know what, and this applies as much to a drawing of something remote in time and place as it does to a drawing at a Motor Show (of which I have done many in the past).

The difference is that when drawing period figures you cannot just go on to the streets and start drawing. This kind of subject calls for in depth research. Go to the public library for books on the period and scour the nearest museum for information. The search for knowledge is a very hard discipline, and all to your own good. Although one ideal is to have a live model with costume, you will find that your drawing from life in your sketch-book will come to your aid when a paid-for model and hired costume are out of the question, and that soon you will be able to draw imaginative figures without recourse to a model.

Here, then, are the steps of working out a finished story illustration. I am using, as an example, a drawing done for the novel *Roderick Random* by Smollett. The scene aimed at will show a guest the worse for drink, being carried from the house and being seen off by the host.

First, a roughed-out sketch, one of two or three tried out aspects. These simple line movements may seem to tell little more than what the action is about, but they are also to help find the broad, general composition and the disposition of the large white and black areas. You may feel it necessary to do two or three roughs before you feel confident in the suitability for the finished drawing. Here is a list of the elements to be put together:

1 A figure at the doorway – the host
2 The tipsy guest being carried off to the sedan chair
3 One chairman holding the drunk's legs
4 A second chairman putting his hat on
5 Another guest supporting him under the arms
6 A suggestion of foliage behind the figures

94

Before we can get very far, there are many things we will need to find out about. Here are some simple notes of hats, coats, shoes and wigs, etc.

95

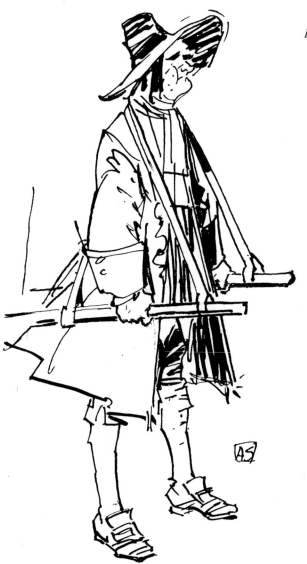

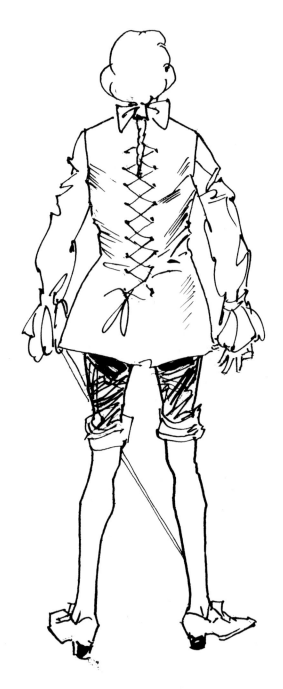

Right You will see here in the finished drawing that, although small changes have taken place (the attitude of the man at the door for instance), the general movements have been adhered to. Notice too, that I had second thoughts and left out the doorsteps of the rough sketch, and, of course, there is no cross-hatching.

Further research would tell us that the chairman figure would not wear a fancy flowered coat, but more probably some coarse and heavier all-weather coat and presumably some gentleman's cast-off. He would also be likely to wear his own hair, rather than a wig, as the latter were expensive and were only worn by the wealthy.

Right Who would have thought that a waistcoat would be tightened up at the back with strings in this way? You may never use the information, but remember the ploughing sketches and how much was discarded?

Here is an exercise in the use of only one instrument – a No. 1 sable brush. There is no pen work here at all. Although this is a book about line drawing, that does not mean that you must draw exclusively with the pen – this is still a line drawing. I have varied the thickness of the line and it's direction to entertain the eye, using also a large area of almost solid black, and a simple flower-like pattern on one of the figures. This, as always, has to be thought about carefully before putting the ink to paper. The varying thicknesses of line and their relationship to the white areas and strong blacks, as you see, give, us a kind of colour.

Another example of 'colour'.
The whole thing was drawn
with a 303 nib, except for the
bold window reflections and
the strong shading on the
man's coat, for which I used
a No. 1 brush.

99

With constant practice with the sketch-book it should be a short step to drawing an imaginative figure without a model. I used this figure from my picture of 'The Jolly Beggars' in the Burns Museum in Irvine. I translated from colour in oils to colour in line, without models remember, but only after much reference to the sketch-book.

Left and bottom When it came to the little mouse, I felt that I had to find out a little more than I knew about mice, and so I went out to look for one. I was lucky enough to find a dead one in the garden, and went to some pains to draw it carefully before condensing it to the little figure that I needed. Much of the information gathered in these sketches was abandoned in the final drawing, as you will see.

Right This drawing is pure invention, without the use of a model, but it gives an idea of how really big areas of black can be used with the brush. But notice that the blacks are never allowed to be totally black: here and there, little lights are allowed to come through. The character of the line is the essence of the whole endeavour, and you will see no cross-hatching here. I dislike cross-hatching, for it is a lazy device and does not take us very far. Colour, imaginative lighting, and the entertainment of the line itself are caught with clear, direct strokes. If your ideas

on how to interpret are muddled, so will the rendering be. Clear thoughts and a decided commitment to the paper are what you must go for. The concentric rings are a device that I hit on for this particular drawing to suggest the light from the lantern across the figure and into the background shadow. Your speedy sketch-book work will help you into this appearance of easy spontaneity. Your energy on the sketch-book pays off.

A similar figure to the previous example, but, this time with straight lines
radiating like the spokes of a wheel. These are not the only two ways of
using the line for lighting effects: experience will prove this.
Here again you will see that no cross-hatching has been used anywhere.

10 Cars and bikes-scenes from everyday life

It is unwise for the artist to become too specialised in one particular field to the exclusion of all else. Cars, bicycles and motor bikes may not be your favourite subjects, but they are all around us in everyday life and you should learn how to tackle them. The slender, almost ethereal line of the bicycle can be contrasted with the rather brutal weight and power of the motor bike, and in drawing one or the other the reaction calls for considerable adjustment in feeling. You may find the idea of drawing a motor bike daunting because of its complexity, but the discipline of looking at something new will bring out your best. On the other hand, you may find you enjoy the challenge such subjects offer and want to make drawings fit for the manufacturer's catalogue. But, even if your drawing is to be no more than an adjunct to a comic caption, the subject has to be investigated and drawn carefully before you take liberties with it in caricature. You need to know as much as possible before you can discard.

One way of putting the bicycle and the motor car together with a little dog for good measure, from our previous practice on dogs. Take special note of the following hints on right-angle ellipses on the car wheels as the steering wheel turns.

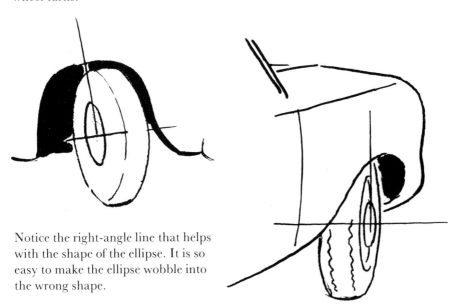

Notice the right-angle line that helps with the shape of the ellipse. It is so easy to make the ellipse wobble into the wrong shape.

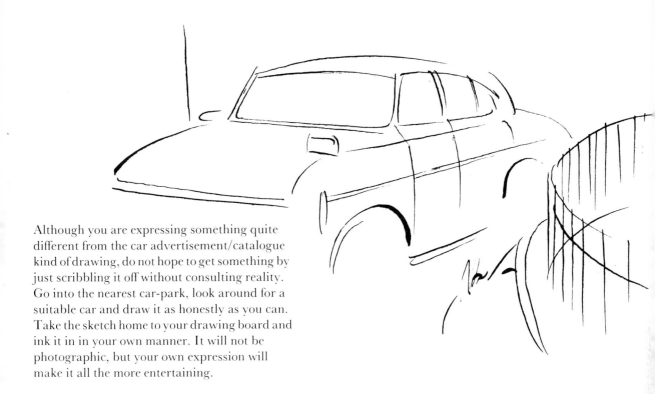

Although you are expressing something quite different from the car advertisement/catalogue kind of drawing, do not hope to get something by just scribbling it off without consulting reality. Go into the nearest car-park, look around for a suitable car and draw it as honestly as you can. Take the sketch home to your drawing board and ink it in in your own manner. It will not be photographic, but your own expression will make it all the more entertaining.

Here, a small preliminary rough sketch. Two or three roughs might be needed to settle the general pattern in your mind. However, you have need again of reference to your sketch-book, for even a pram is an awkward thing to draw without a careful examination of the model. Here I have made no use of either a blockmaker's tint or toothbrush splatter work, but concentrated on pattern, the simplicity of clean lines and an agreeable distribution of blacks and whites.

Have you noticed that when you try to copy your rough sketch on to the finished drawing, the finished attempt is often less good than the rough? This is because, while you may have caught something quite lively in the rough, it will lose some of its spontaneity if copied slavishly. So really, you should try to get up steam all over again and attack it anew. You may permit yourself a glance now and again, but that is all.

Knowing nothing perhaps about motor-
bikes and being puzzled by what you see,
there is only one thing left to do, and that is
to leave it to your eyes. Draw what you see
and, in time, the logic of the structure will
begin to clear itself and you will become
more comfortable and confident.

The first tentative drawing of a
motor-bike in the simplest of
learning lines, with little
attempt at finish: just a simple
getting to know the model,
remembering that the result is
your interpretation of the
subject and not a photographic
catalogue imitation.

For a little composition like this, make one or two trial runs on odd scraps of paper and, having satisfied yourself as to the arrangement, go and find a model, and, if possible, a friendly mechanic who is prepared to stand, or take an attitude beside it, for a few minutes to help you with the relationships and proportions.

11 The comic strip

There is no question that the comic strip gives a lot of pleasure. I remember being told that the daily paper for which I drew after the war, sold more than four million copies every morning, which meant an eager comic strip readership of about ten million. The term comic strip covers a very wide range of expression. From the extravagantly comic figure of the 'Pop Eye' type, to the carefully detailed figures and contrivances of the science-fiction characters: it is quite obvious, even in this field of art, that every artist expresses himself differently and is at once recognised by his devoted fans. The creator will take a pride in his work and love his characters. After all, they are unique and quite his own.

The characters I have used here are of a small boy and his cat, which I invented and drew for some years in a weekly London magazine. One has to be quite ingenious, for it is not as simple as it looks, to put over an idea in only three pictures and no captions. But this kind of invention does come with practice. As you will see, the first need in this kind of strip is to reduce the characters and background to the simplest possible formula. Your original drawings could be drawn one and a half times the size of the final reproduction; a good size this, as it holds the original feeling of the line. The more serious, story-telling strips, such as the space adventure, the love story serial for teenagers, and the western, call for more research, which is in itself always an interesting occupation.

Drawing in pen and ink can have very simple aims, or very complicated ones. The kind of problems the artist faces when he wishes to suggest atmosphere, strong sun, lights and shadows, foliage, the texture of polished wood, a bunch of flowers ablaze with colour, are not likely to worry us too much in the type of comic strip on this page. But, the comic strip is not to be despised for its simplicity. If well done, it can give pleasure to millions. It is a fact that Picasso was an avid fan of the American weekly comic strip supplements and had a real sympathy with the comic drawing, and how many more painters, quietly, are just as fond of these comic drawings?

If your drawings are going to appear daily in a newspaper (this does not apply of course to the topical cartoon) you will be expected to have a supply for a month or six weeks ready in advance to cover any contingency (you might catch cold or want to go for a holiday.) If the strip is of the story-telling serial kind, you will probably have the assistance of a worker already on the staff of the paper or someone of your own choosing, perhaps a freelance like yourself. If you are able to write your own plots, so much the better.

All drawing is one, and although the comic strip looks so different in manner from the drawing of the figure being carried to the sedan chair on p.97, it is only an adjustment of your mental attitude to the different feeling that you want to express. Your skill with the pencil and constant practice of inking in (once again, never with cross-hatching) will carry you through.

The little boy with his cat.

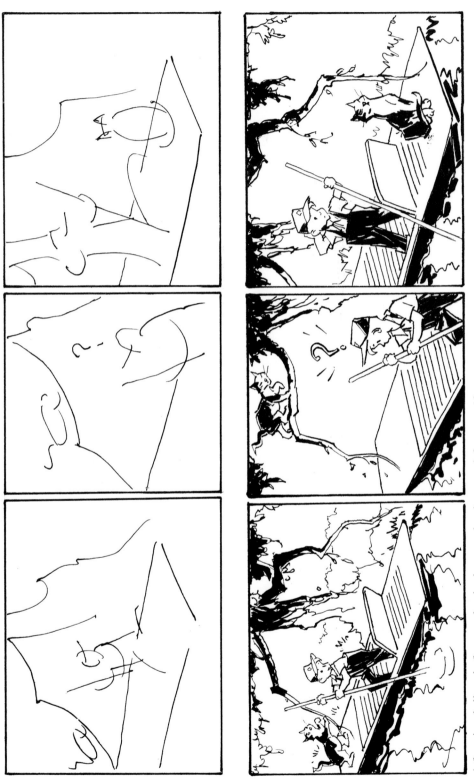

A few simple lines before you begin the actual strip, to satisfy yourself as to where the elements will be placed to put the story over and, remember, the simpler the layout the better. These were pencil lines, of course, inked in for clarity. This feature, as it happens, was for a children's page, but was at the same time used in foreign papers. The advantage of not having captions or speech balloons is that most strips can be used anywhere without the trouble of translation.

The following examples show two ways of putting across the same idea, perhaps to suit different editorial needs. The second one has been protracted to four pictures with lettering in balloons. The half-tone effect is achieved by means of a blockmaker's tint and is indicated with a light wash of Prussian Blue watercolour on the original drawing.

12 The pen and ink artist

Pen versus paintbrush

Most people consider the pen and ink artist to be somewhat inferior to the painter, but a comparison of the two is not really valid. It is like comparing the cheetah with the horse; it is like saying 'Yes, he is a fine carpenter, but what a pity he did not become an electrician.' As often as not, the best of landscape painters is a poor portrait painter and vice versa. Each artist is confined within his own nature and that is what it finally comes down to.

This reminds me of George Whitelaw, a pen and ink artist of front rank who drew for *Punch* amongst other weeklies, and who, as a student, got a dressing down from the principal of the Glasgow Art School. Whitelaw was working on a drawing in pen an ink (this was taboo) and the shocked voice over his shoulder said: 'What! Are you going to be a hack artist then?' Well, Whitelaw had no impulse to be a painter, and how much better for him, and for all those who have admired his clever drawings since, that he followed his nature and stuck to black and white.

When I myself went to art school, the tutor, seeing me drawing in pen and ink said: 'One day you will have your fill of that.' I have done a great number of black and white drawings since, and a great many paintings, and I will always have a soft spot for the black line on white paper.

Painting can often be effective, meritricious and attractively showy, but hide the want of good drawing, proper perspective, good rhythms and the poetry of balanced movement. The wide opportunities open to the painter are closed to the pen and ink artist. It should be remembered that he is an impressionist and, more impressionistic than any painter ever was, he will learn the need for an intelligent and sharp understanding of the limitations and scope of his medium. He must develop the power of telling his message in as few lines as possible, each stroke being absolutely and uniquely necessary, even though the lines may appear to have been struck off in an easy, inspired way. He will know that it is never quite as easy as that, and that each line must be carefully thought about before the slightest mark appears on the paper. And it is not an easy skill to come by – to be able to suggest everything that comes to the eye, from the colour in a bunch of carnations to the tinge of an infant's cheek.

I, then, draw with pen and ink as a change from the problems of painting, not because it is any easier. It is as difficult as any other medium to master; it's just that the problems are different. In many ways it is more difficult than painting: there are no lucky accidents of which one can take advantage, as there are in watercolour painting, nor the quick showy results that even a beginner will often achieve in oils.

Naturally, you will follow your inclination and do what you are happiest at. The artist has the need to discover himself and, in order to recognise his potential, he might well be subject to fads and changing impulses. As already stated, I myself have painted and sold all kinds of paintings as well as my work in pen an ink. In fact, I think it is useful exercise for the pen and ink artist to practise now and again painting in oils. In some mysterious way, the use of the brush is of great help to the handling of the pen. This reinforces my belief, that all drawing is, in fact, one. But if you have a comic turn of mind, the cartoon and the comic strip will be a natural outlet for you. In many comic strips the artist may collaborate with a script-writer or 'ideas' man, but anyone can cultivate the knack of coming up with a comic strip to order. It comes with practice, I can assure you. I have done it so many times and have never collaborated on a comic strip.

It is also worth remembering that it is only a recent attitude towards art that the artist must express himself in some esoteric way or else he is no artist. Self expression is obviously important, but one should bear in mind that the artist of the past practised as an honest tradesman (his work is still held in high regard) and, therefore, needed to find a patron.

Whether he produced work for the church or painted portraits for the rich merchant and his family, he was on commission for the work he produced.

The important point is that no two artists of any standing today, or at any time in the past, have ever imitated one another in their expression or manner. It is essential to obey your own nature, and not to be overwhelmed by someone else – be yourself. Every artist has his own way of using the nib, and each achieves his own style, often after much labour, but when he does, there is no mistaking his own individual touch. Just as the envelope on the mat, seen even at a distance, tells us who wrote the address, so with the black and white artist; and the one sure way of arriving at facility is inking in, in your sketch-book. However, you should not aim specifically to acquire a manner. Individually is a by-product of practice. Self-consciousness – seeking for style – is affectation. Just aim to get a sincerely good drawing and the style will look after itself.

For the mathematician, two and two will always make four, whether he is measuring astronomical distance or tiny areas under a microscope; and one chemical formula will apply as much for one chemist as for another; one lawyer, too, knows as well as another what the law can do and what it cannot. All this knowledge has been laboriously gathered and built upon by generations past, but there are no such absolute, fixed rules for the artist to work within. He must make his own equations (compensation for imbalance), and develop his own language. He is equally bound as is the mathematician to his laws. As with the composer of music or the poet, the artist's doings are inspired by mysterious forces from within, where precedent or ready-made formulae help but little. Each painting is the product of the artist's imagination and skill, and each is a revelation of his own unique nature.

It was as a contributor to one of Odhams old weeklies that I met Illingworth, some years my senior, also a contributor. The painstaking excellence of his drawing was so overwhelming that my own drawings seemed careless beside them. One day, the editor sent for me and, holding up one of my earlier contributions, said: 'That is what I want from you, not this,' pointing to a recent drawing which had an obvious new influence. How wrong I had been. He explained that the seemingly easy spontaneity of the first drawing was what I should deliver. Briefly, he was saying, 'be yourself'.

Another lesson comes to mind. Years after that experience, Frank Patterson's beautiful landscapes in pen and ink were appearing in another publication simultaneously with my own. I knew that I could never match Patterson in the landscape line, and I shrank from the attempt. One day the editor came to me and said: 'Frank Patterson wants to meet you.' He showed me his letter from which it was obvious that he admired my work as much as I did his. This taught me the lesson again: not to yearn after the unattainable – that which is not in your nature – but to cultivate your own resources. So, be yourself. Work at it. Fill your sketch-books, ink in your sketches and you will find your own style will appear by itself. It was said of Phil May that 'he drew as a bird sings'. Draw from 'life' every day in your sketch-book, and you will be on the way to creating your own, individual song.

Potential markets

There are many outlets for pen and ink drawings. Every daily newspaper uses line drawings in one way or another. The weeklies, too, have their share of line drawings, either as illustrations or in the comic strip pages, not forgetting the many advertisers who need the line drawing to sell their products.

Some publishers specialise in books for junior readership, from the fairy-tale, comic type of drawing, to a quite seriously instructive kind of line work, often calling for considerable research. Artists will often specialise in quite a narrow age group, perhaps between the ages of four and six years, or seven to ten, and so on upwards to the older teenagers.

Reprints of the classics are very often illustrated by line artists as are travel books, biographies, and historical books (although nowadays novels are rarely illustrated). Childrens magazines and annuals, of course, keep a large number of artists busy.

Pen artists to study

At this point, I should like to mention some great pen and ink artists very well worth studying. They call for our admiration and perhaps, too, can give us instruction. Go to your public library and ask the librarian to help you find them.

1 Phil May who drew for *Punch* around the 1890s. His drawings were very free, and done with apparent natural ease, with a fresh and lively pen style, although it is known that he put in a lot of hard work to get the seemingly easy results.

2 Charles Keene, also in *Punch*. As a draughtsman, he was among the greatest with his pen. His drawings have been published again in recent years in book form, showing the true value of his line and draughtsmanship.

3 Howard Pyle, a great American illustrator who drew for *Harpers* magazine and also for Scribners. Like the previously mentioned artist, he was active at the end of the nineteenth century and his illustrations are among the best in the history of drawing.

4 Illingworth of *Punch*. Perhaps the best in pure draughtsmanship in recent times. His genius lies in a painstaking attention to detail.

5 Daniel Urrabieta Vierge, a Spaniard of the 1880s and 1890s. He illustrated the book *Pablo de Segovia* by Quivedo, among many other things. How he could evoke the hot Spanish sun on his figures and buildings! And all just with a pen line. If ever you feel that your progress is too slow, spare a thought for Vierge who had to begin all over again in middle life after paralysis hit his right hand. He had to re-learn to draw with his left. He triumphed. So, take courage.

Investigate them all. They will give you much pleasure. They will show up, too, the degeneracy of much of the material in modern magazines and the monotony of the photographic themes seen on the bookstalls.

I should also like to mention two very fine artists with the pen, who drew for the long defunct *Passing Show* from 1920 to 1928: Leo Cheney and Gilbert Wilkinson. Volumes at Odhams Press were destroyed in the Blitz, but it may be that somewhere there is another record of their work and that they will surface again one day.

You may wonder why I have not included in this book, specimen reproductions of other line artists. The point is that if 1000 aspiring pen artists applied themselves conscientiously to the study of black and white line work, you would see ultimately 1000 different 'fists', as in handwriting and, simply to follow any one of the half dozen or so artists it might have been possible to show here, would not really serve any useful purpose. At the risk of repeating myself, your own manner will come by itself by filling one sketch-book after another and inking in your pencil drawings for hours every day.

Remember at all times that the line can never imitate the elements that are in your drawing: it represents them and reminds the spectator of them in a new and entertaining way. What have been the most important points to learn in these pages? Practise drawing hands, carry your sketch-book with you at all times and *think before you ink!*